IT'S ABOUT THE JOURNEY,

THE LESSONS LEARNED:

NOT THE DESTINATION!

Oh, to hear your whispered promise
Once more.
The caress of your breath
Snaking its grip around my neck.
Feeding my soul with pleasure,
I'd gladly succumb to temptation.

It isn't a choice I now have.

I see your face in every stranger I meet
It's the hope that you cross my path
Again...
To see the eyes that know my soul,
The ones that complete me.
The ones that make me whole.
That see into the void inside,
And fill up the emptiness
You willingly left behind.

The stars no longer guide me.

The night sky has become a torment of a million thousand
regrets.
The darkness is suffocating and all encompassing,

Existing in thoughts of why I wasn't enough.

When you walked away,
You took the best part of me with you...

My heart and my love.

I will always yearn for
The missed kiss,
The missed dances,
The missed dates,
The missed opportunities,
The missed laughter,
The missed love.

But most of all...

I miss YOU.

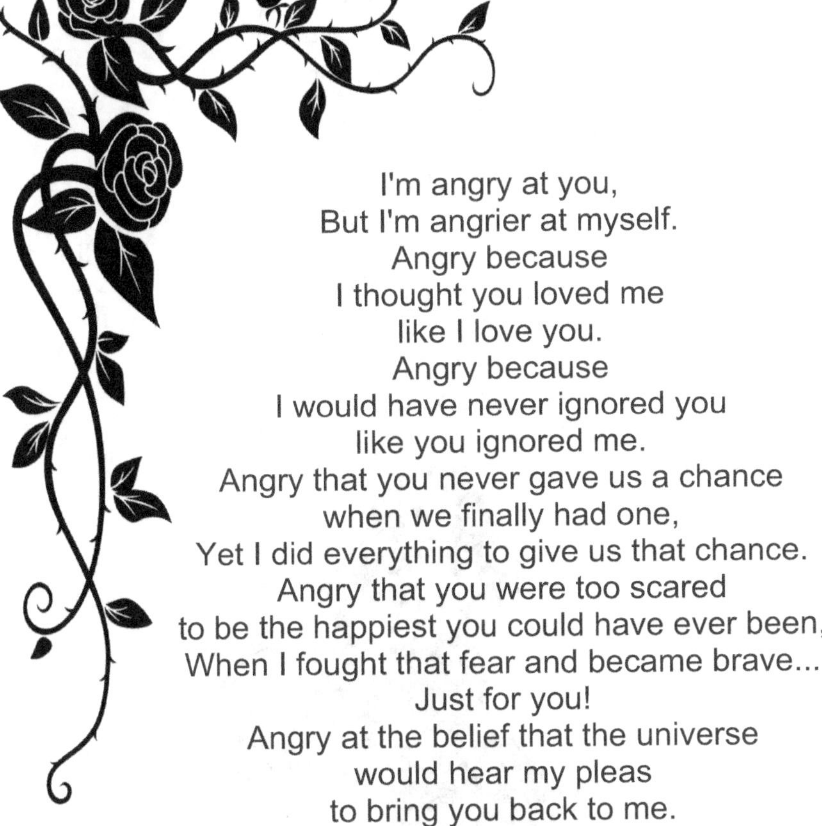

I'm angry at you,
But I'm angrier at myself.
Angry because
I thought you loved me
like I love you.
Angry because
I would have never ignored you
like you ignored me.
Angry that you never gave us a chance
when we finally had one,
Yet I did everything to give us that chance.
Angry that you were too scared
to be the happiest you could have ever been,
When I fought that fear and became brave...
Just for you!
Angry at the belief that the universe
would hear my pleas
to bring you back to me.
Angry that I may never feel what I felt when I was with you.

Oh, it was the promises you made,
The promise of what was to be,
What was to come...
I never knew.
But I always lived in hope.
Hope that you'd see me,
Hope that you would choose me...
But you didn't,
You saw me and still
You didn't choose me.
So now,
I choose myself!

No beauty shined as bright
As mine did through your eyes,
The windows to the soul of our universe
The enchanted mirror that I saw myself in.
It's utterly heart-breaking
that you never knew that...

I saw in you in that most magical of ways too.

Just one moment needs to happen.

Just one spectacular moment is required
Where I see you
You see me

Time falls away
And we are reunited.

Forever.

We spent an age searching for each other,
We were lost to others.
Then found one another again...
Why, when time has gifted us another chance,
Haven't we grasp what was meant for us

All along?

I'm in a relationship with you
Even though I'm not.
I'm in love with you
Even though I don't want to be.
I'm tied to you,
Even though I want to be free.
I'm forever yours,
Even if you don't want to be mine.

Can you feel the pull,
Like I can?
Do you dream of me,
Like I do of you?
Do you try to forget,
Knowing you can't?
Like I have tried?
Have you given up?

Because I never will!

I want to spend the rest of my sunrises with you.
In the place where so many others visit
But which we call our own.
I want to start each day in your arms,
In the place that I call home.

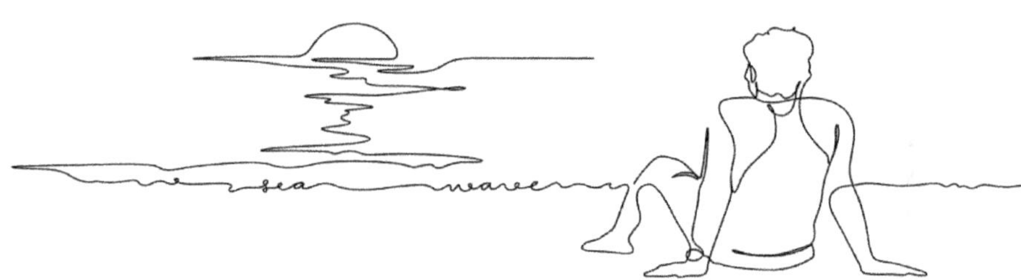

I ran
Just as you are now.
The confusion overwhelming,
Emotions flitting
between heartbreak and hatred.
Towards you,
At me.
Now it's clear,
Simple and true...
We both lived in fear.

I am so alone,
I am so lonely.
But I would rather be this
And wait a thousand lifetimes
For you,
My love.
Rather than enter a mockery,
A fake mimicking love...
Because you,
To me:

Are irreplaceable.

My soul is tied to you,
I've tried to free it...
I really, really have.
I've argued, pleaded, cried,
Threatened, promised:
The stubborn spirit within me,
I fear, may never be able
To let you go.
To move on.
What that means for me...

I do not know.

Sneaking into my dreams,
Terrorising my feelings.
Complicating my emotions,
Killing my progress...

Killing my healing.

You are perfect,
My soulmate.
The one, single person
That completely matches me in every way.

Complimenting my ideals and morals,
Challenging me to be a better version
Of myself.
Without criticism or pressure.
Making me love myself,
Seeing who I truly am
And loving me completely.
You asked for nothing in return.
Nothing.

Why?

I cannot not write you,
I try...

But you are
And always will be,

My leading man.

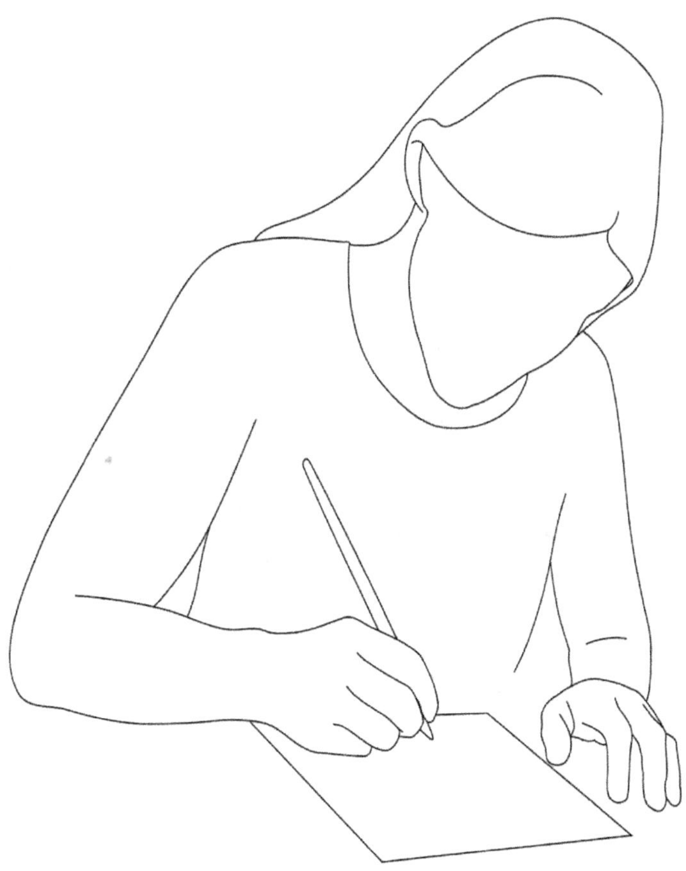

I'm fighting to end our fairy-tale,
The right way.

What are you doing?

Are you fighting as hard as I am?

Or should I give up...

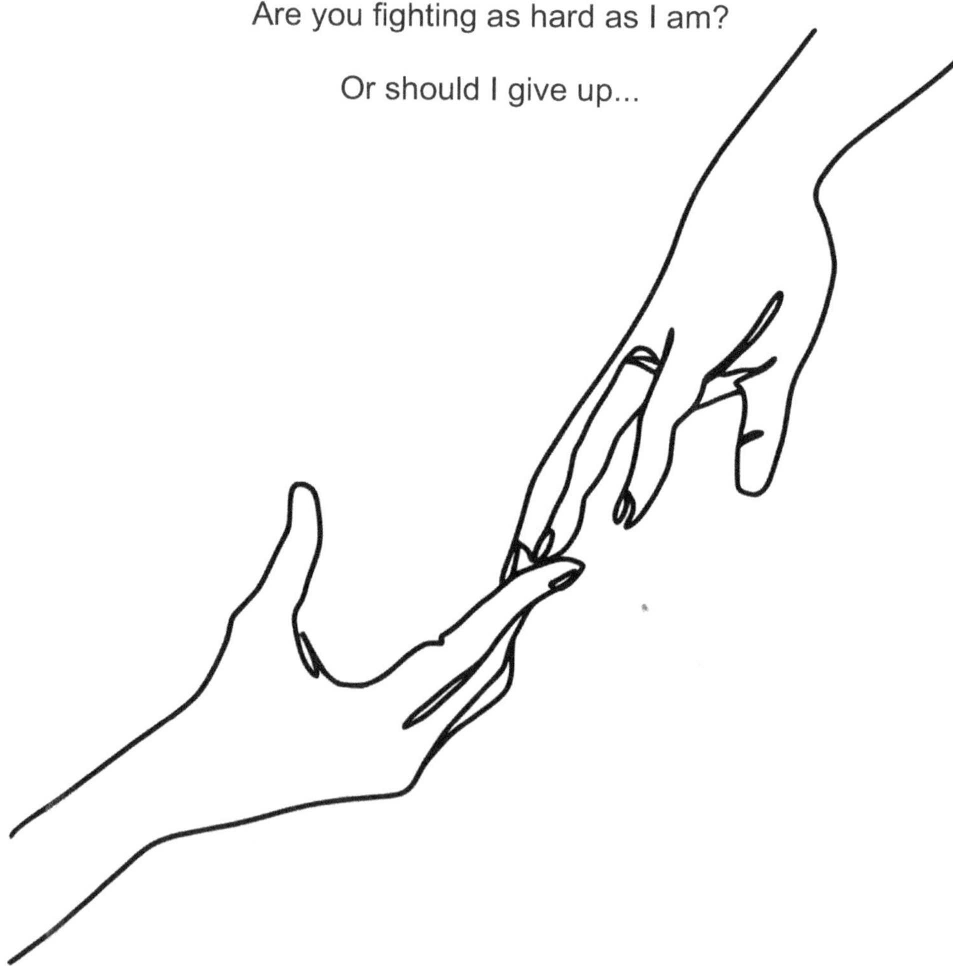

If this isn't love
Then why...
Even when we're not together,
Does it feel better
Than anything I've ever felt?

I have loved you
From the moment I saw you.
The inexplicable feeling
Of already knowing you
But not really knowing you at all.
The magnetic pull that said,
"It's them, they're the ONE."
I have tried,
I have done everything I can
But nothing stops the truth,
That you are my ONE,
You are my ONLY.
I see it all so clearly now.
I just wished that you did as well.

Do you manage to forget about me?
Even just for a moment?
Do you find solace and comfort in the arms of another?
Only to then realise that my arms are the only ones
you ever want wrapped around your waist.
I know in the quiet places,
In the silence,
That it's me that you think of...
Just as I think of you.

What a waste of life and love we are!
The fear of being unloved has won,
The stubbornness of us both
Has beaten all bravery.
What a shameful pair we are:
To push away the signs,
To ignore our intuition,
To say no to feelings.

No wonder...

We don't deserve this love at all!

It's been so long
That I'm starting to think I dreamt you up.
That you don't exist,
You're a figment of my imagination.
That nothing was real,
My mind is playing a trick.
This thought alone,
Makes me feel sick.

I know I will be your last true love,
Even if I won't be with you till your last days.
That's a truly painful thought to admit.

I know you are mine,
Bound by eternity.
Bound by fate
Bound by destiny:
Tied forever more
By the endless universe.
It was decided long ago.

What am I supposed to do with all this love?
All this love that I have inside,
For you!
I can't move on,
I can't give it to someone else.
I can't even lavish it on myself:

So, it just sits here,
In my heart.
Just wasting away...

Just like me.

When I look back,
When I reflect on my life...
I see there was balance at times,
Moments of true satisfaction.
Those moments were fleeting,
And they only happened
When you were present.
I now realise that you were that
Balance,
You were the missing piece.
You will always be the one,
The one that kept me:

Balanced.

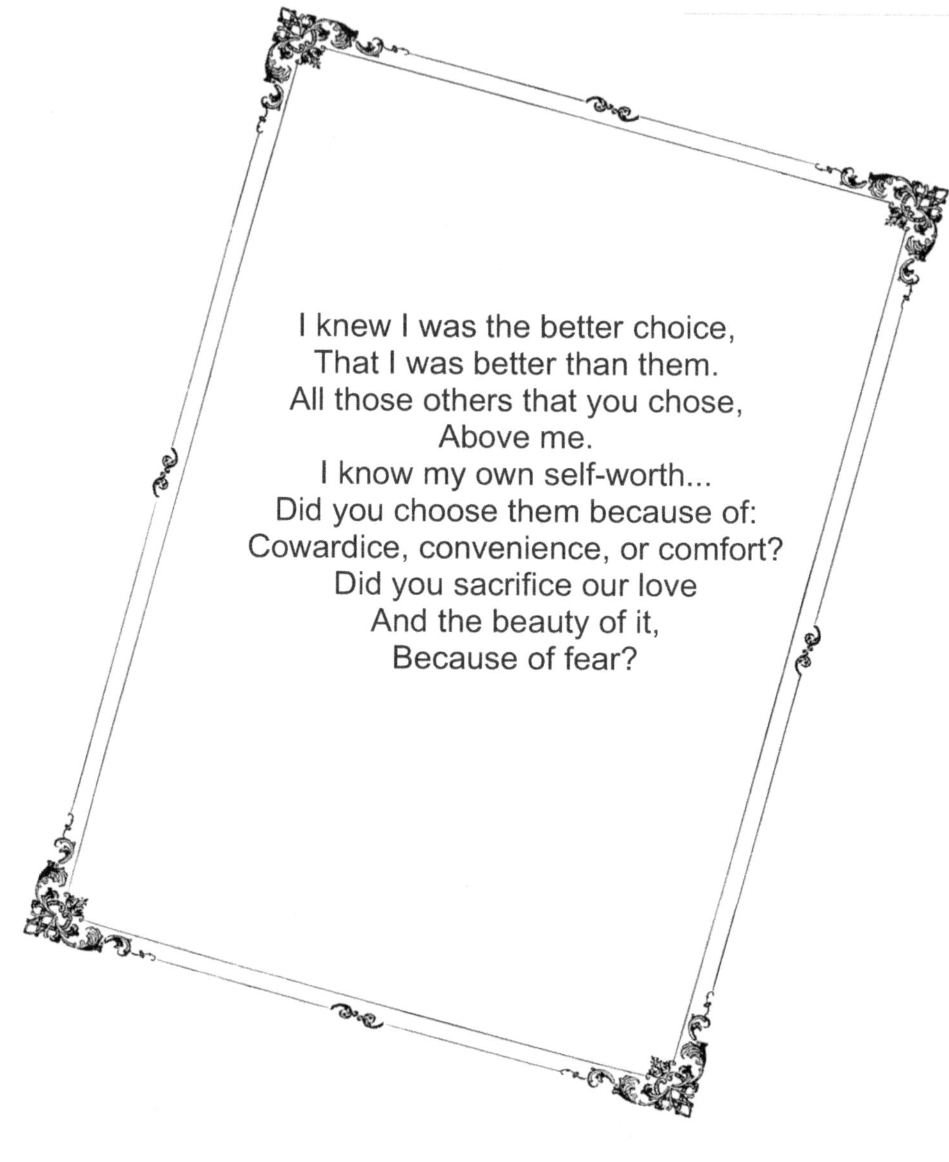
I knew I was the better choice,
That I was better than them.
All those others that you chose,
Above me.
I know my own self-worth...
Did you choose them because of:
Cowardice, convenience, or comfort?
Did you sacrifice our love
And the beauty of it,
Because of fear?

When I think of you,
I am never sad or upset.
Even though we are apart,
All I think of is how you make me feel.
I only ever smile,
It doesn't matter that you didn't choose me.
What matters is...
I only have beautiful memories of us.

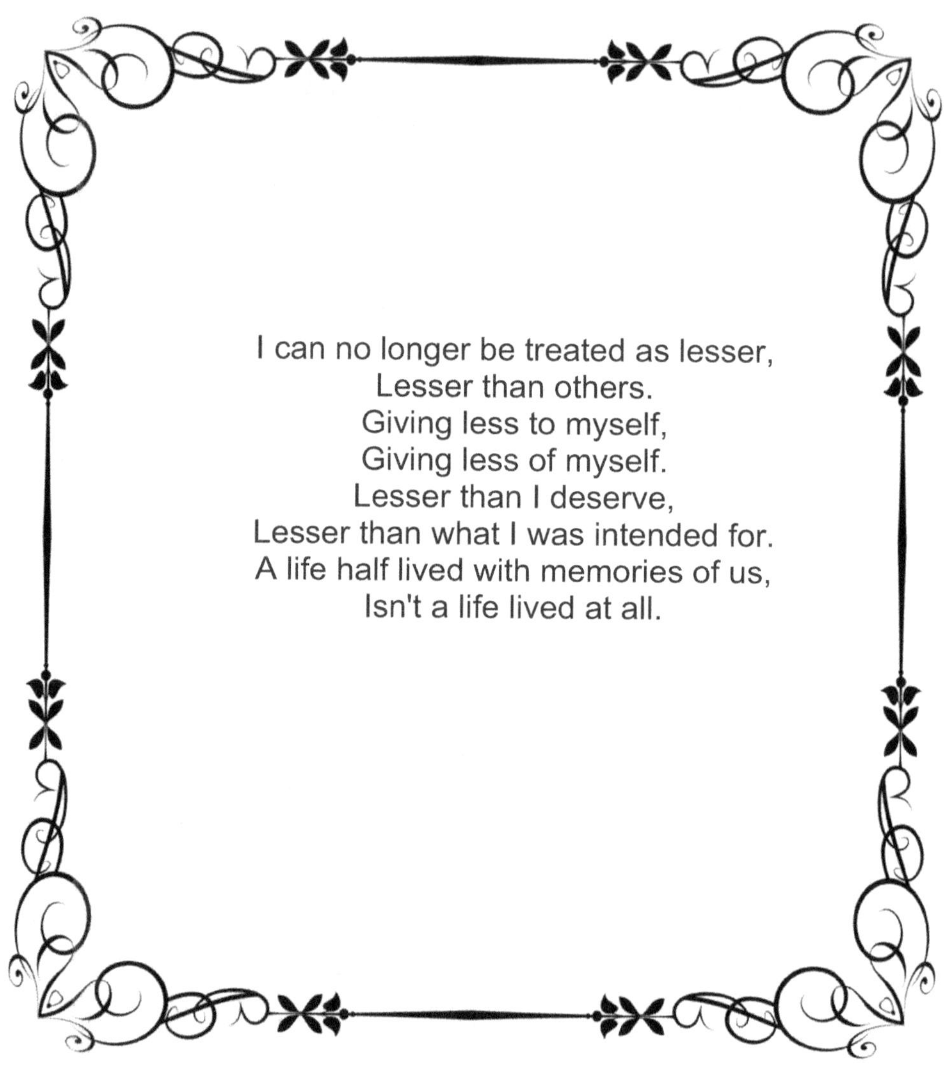
I can no longer be treated as lesser,
Lesser than others.
Giving less to myself,
Giving less of myself.
Lesser than I deserve,
Lesser than what I was intended for.
A life half lived with memories of us,
Isn't a life lived at all.

I am so consumed by you,
So consumed by too many what ifs.
I know I have the strength to get through this,
I need to overcome this attachment.
Step by step,
Slowly through this storm of pain.
To see a glimmer of light,
Leading me to an everlasting love
Where I never have to question myself:

EVER AGAIN!

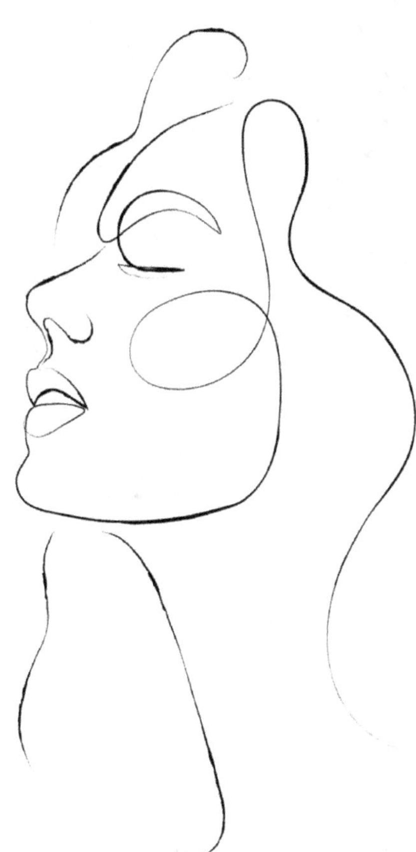

I tried to understand you,
I tried to make excuses for you.
I tried to make you want me,
I tried to never ignore you.

Trying got me your attention
But no matter how hard I tried...

It was never enough.

I'm glad I Loved you,
That you knew it clearly.
That I never wavered in my emotions
Or expression of them.
I glad that you were able to have the comfort that I never did.
You never had to question my love
And I'd offer it all to you again and again.
I rather love you too much
Than ever cause you any pain.

Your resistance to Us
Was the real villain
It murdered our chance of happiness.
It whispered to you so quietly,
It made sure I didn't hear.
It preyed on your weakness
And you obeyed Willingly.

I deserved you telling me you loved me.
I deserved you showing me you loved me.
I deserved you making time for me.
I deserved your affection.
I deserved a response when I poured out my soul.

And you gave me silence.

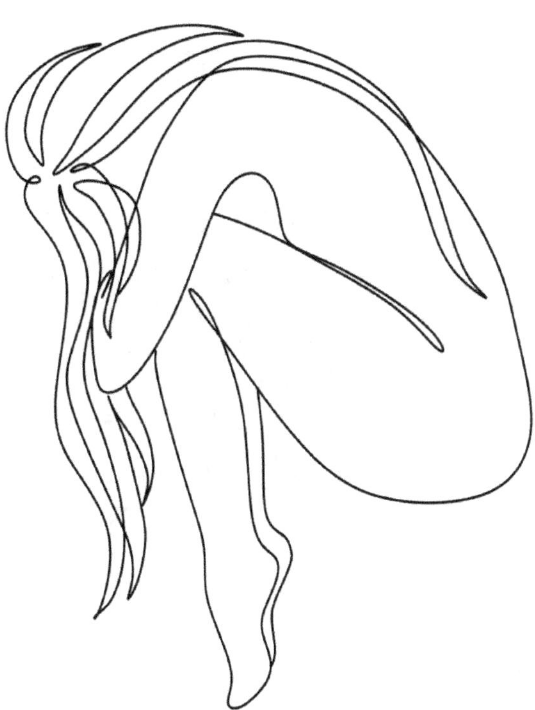

I've been depriving myself of love
For so, so long.
In the hopes that you will finally gift me
Some of your love.
The blinkers are now lifted,
I see you:
For you.
I will always love you
But I can no longer wait,
For nothing...

Not anymore.

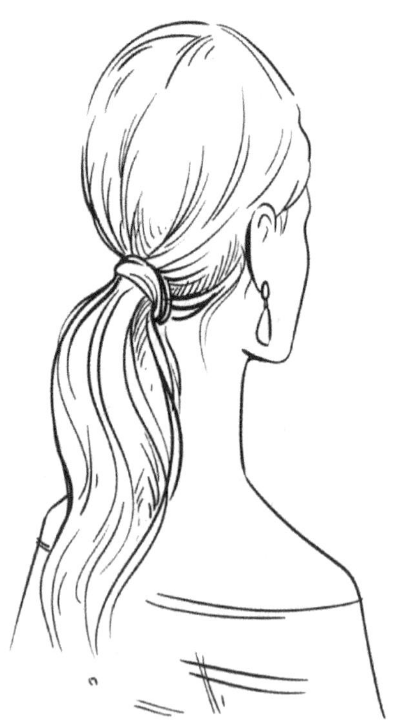

I often ponder what scared you...
Was it me?
Was it all of me?
Was it just a part of me?
Was it the thought of us?
Was it us in general?
Or...
Was it you?
Just you?
Timid and afraid of love,
Running from the possibility of being truly happy?

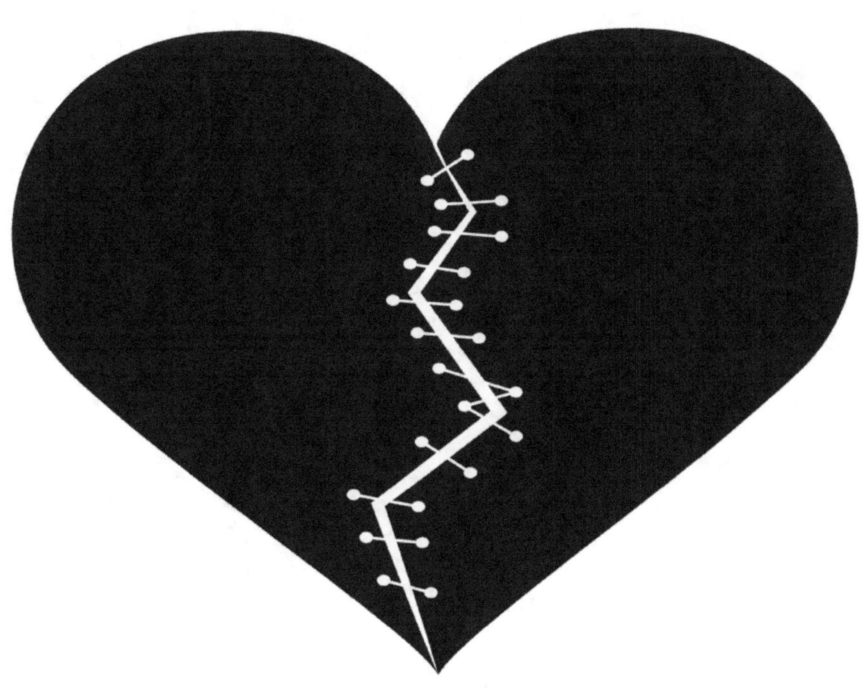

Sabotage yourself,
Sabotage me.
Sabotage what we were going to be.
A semblance remains of what we were:
Individually and together.
Constant cycles
As if we were the weather!
You are the rain
And I the sun.
I will bring the rainbow
After your Sabotage is done.

I know I'm better than what you offered,
I know I'm better than anything you gave.
I know I'm deserving...
Yet I took the seconds,
The second helpings of someone else's love,
The leftovers of what you had left.
I was never your main,
And I starved myself on your scraps.
Even though you gorged on the feast
I laid out each, and every time!

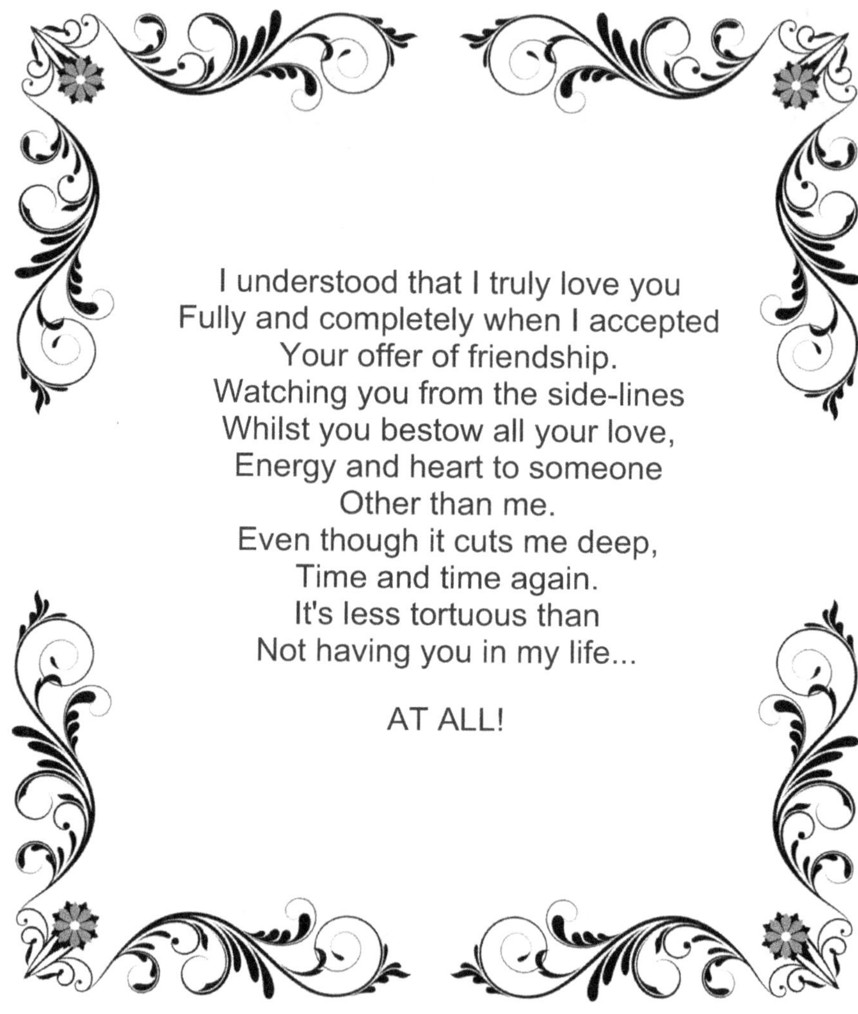

I understood that I truly love you
Fully and completely when I accepted
Your offer of friendship.
Watching you from the side-lines
Whilst you bestow all your love,
Energy and heart to someone
Other than me.
Even though it cuts me deep,
Time and time again.
It's less tortuous than
Not having you in my life...

AT ALL!

What a wicked Web we've weaved,
With all the secrets we've hidden
Up our sleeve.
Deny, distract,
Avoid, backtrack.
It was only going to end up in heartbreak,
I didn't know that it was going to be mine.
I was completely unaware of becoming your 'mistake'.

My conflicting emotions
Ebb and flow like the waves
We waded in.
Sadness, sorrow, frustration...
Immense love: all crashing
Against each other.
Fighting for the shore,
Foaming at the sand.
In its beauty there is so much pain.

It's the sheer belief in romance that I have
and cannot let go of.
It's the want of you telling me
you cannot let me go.
It's the need of you having
to have me in your life.
It's the faith that you will realise
that I am all that you need.
It's the dream that we are meant to be...
It's always the hope.

You seem so confident and sure,
Appearing to be fulfilled and satisfied
To the outside world.
Yet I know your darkness, your inner being,
Even when I know nothing of the demons you carry.
I never needed to know,
You were happy in the patience I offered.
Comfortable in the knowledge of never being judged
with your disclosures.

I was your safety and you

let me float away on the wind.

This, is why you cannot let me fully go...

I'm the only one who never wanted
anything from you.
Not a single material thing.
I wished only to join in the love we shared.
I only ever wanted to make you laugh,
I wanted to just simply love you for being all flawed and
complicated...

Just as I am.
To bring out the hidden spirits in each other.

As we always did.

I know that not a single moment that we spent together was wasted.

Not a drop.

It was Wild.
It was Lived.
It was Serenity
It was Free.
It was Empowering.
It was Bliss.
It was Simplicity
It was Beauty...

It was Love.

I'm in pain.
This isn't black and white.
It's the greyest part of life.
To wonder what it would be like
To be truly loved by you.
Where I'm the heart of your world.
Where together means You and Me.
But I'm not...
Instead, I'm in agony
And my world is just grey.
There is no rainbow here,
There is only wondering.

Breathing life into each other,
Creating an alternate reality.
Making our own rules,
Pretending that we
Were all that existed.
Being something else
To the expected...

Was the most unexpected thing to happen,
of all.

Even now,
When I am told I have all the answers
I need.
I find myself asking,
Puzzling,
Questioning:
Why must I overthink so much?

So now I surrender,
I submit,
I will focus on myself
But...

I will never ever quit!

Tears roll,
Incomplete from my soul.
Torn heart,
Cut and shred apart.
Nightmares interwoven with dreams,
Only the twilight hours hear my screams.
I try to reach for the seas of calm,
That which you:
Call your arms.

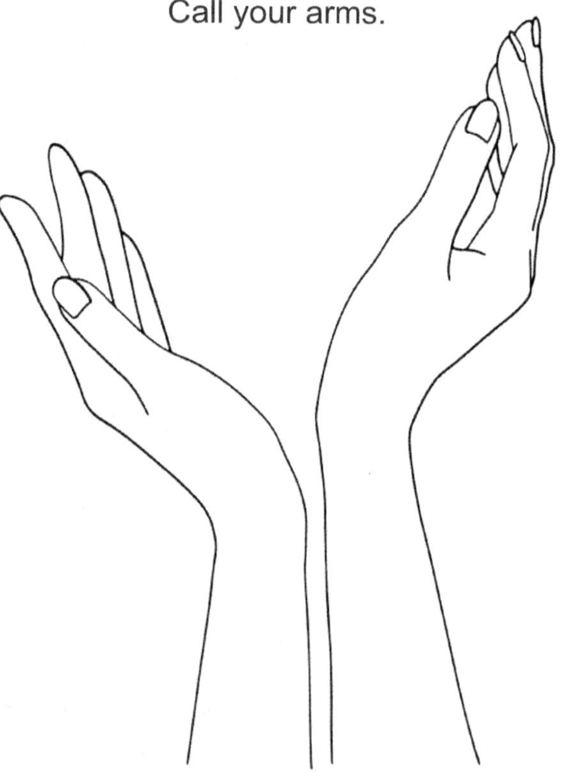

Bleeding emotions
Pouring from every pore
Of my soul.
Darker than the colour of the midnight sky.
Turbulent and violent,
I try to fight them.
I lose every time.
I am lost.
What is to become of me,
I do not know.

Dying life,
Painful laughter,
Friendly knife.
Restraining freedom,
In my dystopian kingdom.
Existing in an oxymoronic state,
Bound by love and hate.

Set me free,
Just let me be!
Why can't it be
Just you and me?
I cannot explain
Why my love
Will not wain.
Promise me this...
That by sacrificing me,
That your life was pure bliss!
That you do not regret
Turning your back on
True love's first and last kiss.

Trembling fear,
Hidden in corners.
Pushed away and overcome.
Conquered demons,
Except one.
Hidden in angelic wings,
With a voice that sings
To me:
'Never let me go...'

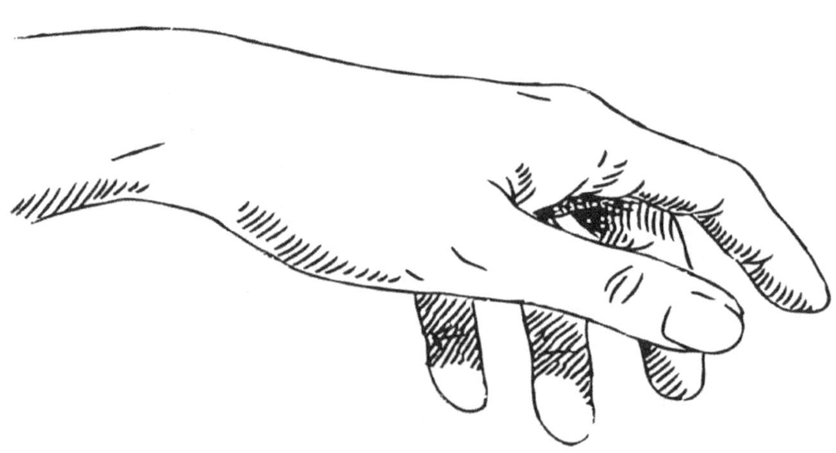

I'm letting go,
Not because I want to.
Not because I need to,
Nor because I must.

I'm letting go...

Because you already left.

No matter the drift
Or the wide ocean between.
You will always appear in my every dream,
Silence now happens more often
Than not,
That's what happens when we settle
For less than our lot.
It hurts
But we'll heal.
Our souls will meet and reflect,
That was the deal.
To teach each other something new
In this lifetime.

Pain, Urges.
Lesson emerges.
Temptation,
Realisation.
Desire, fate.
Can't have,
Too late.
Acceptance,
For my…

Lost soulmate.

I think of you
Every day and night,
I never wanted to give you up
The timing wasn't right.
And yet now when the universe
Has corrected its mistake,
It's the chance of happiness
You will never take!
It's the hardest lesson I've had to learn:
It's a lesson I wished you didn't make.

Why did you always think there was something better?
People spend a lifetime seeking what we had,
It drives me insane
It drives me mad.
Now the binding ties we have
Are almost severed.
Is this the outcome that you always endeavoured?
One lone soul
Outcast from love,
Suffering from never being whole.

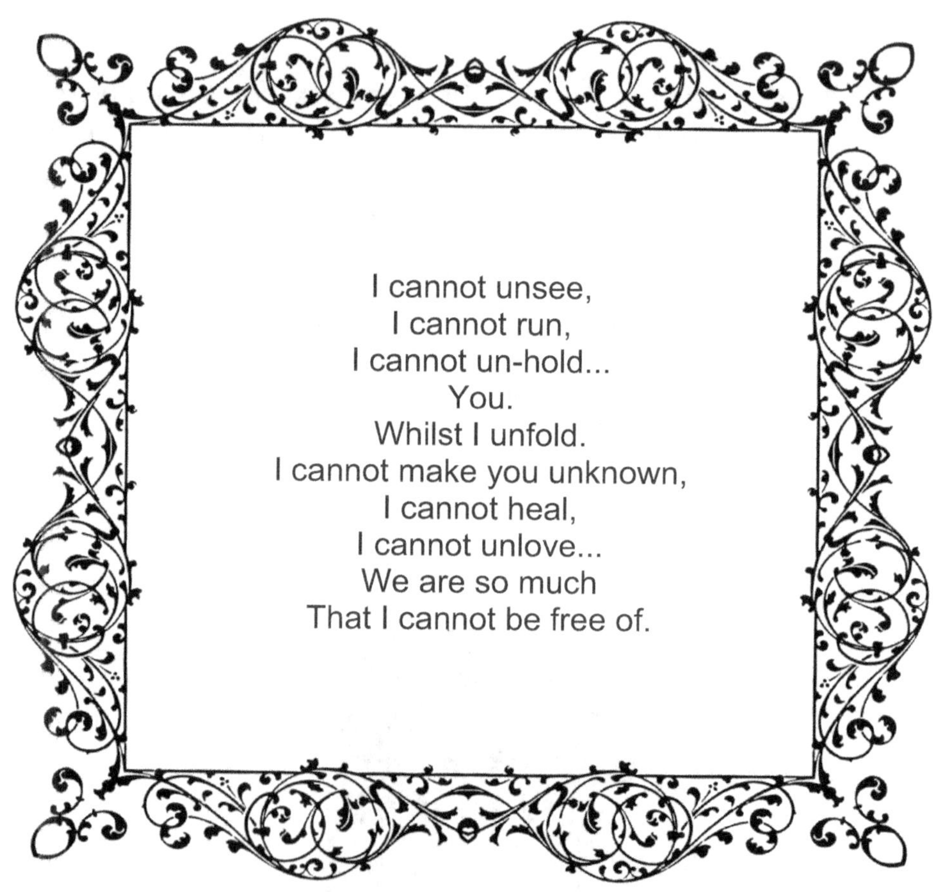
I cannot unsee,
I cannot run,
I cannot un-hold...
You.
Whilst I unfold.
I cannot make you unknown,
I cannot heal,
I cannot unlove...
We are so much
That I cannot be free of.

I'm sick of being lost,
I just want to be free
Either with or without you.
My years wasting away,
Fighting this sickness
Each, and every day.
I am beginning to live with it.
But every day I still wait.

We are a beautiful disaster
Such a perfect mistake.
Stunningly destructive
With just a hint of forbidden love.
What a recipe for utter heartbreak,
That I will always want to indulge in
Time and time again.
It's the only thing that has ever fed my soul.

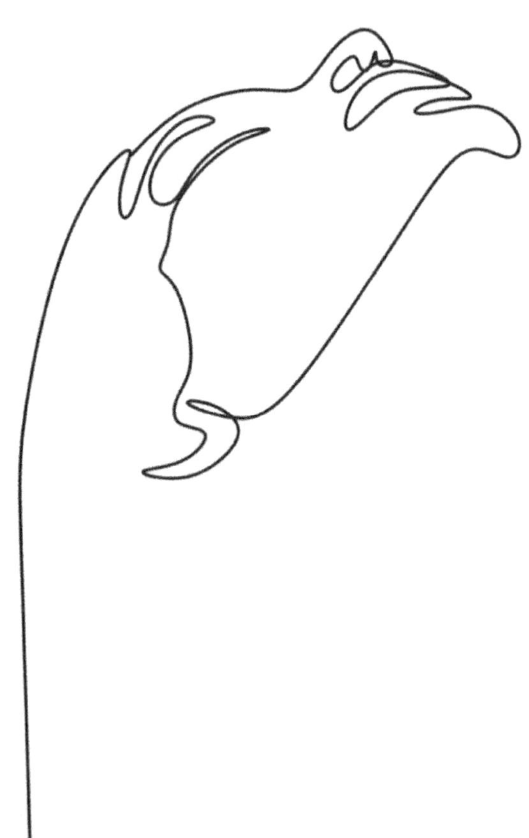

The teasing, the jokes.
The not so innocent strokes.
The push and pull of our connection.
Whilst we go in different directions.
Doesn't take away
And never replaces
The meaning of us as forever and always.

Life wasn't kind to us
So now, all I wish for...

Is for you to remember us
In the light that I do.

You will look everywhere for me,
Just like I did for you.
As I leave you behind
To carry on with your life.
And you will watch from the side-lines,
After you broke me into fragments,
As I rise like the beauty of life
That I am.
Showing the world and you
That I am all the spectacular uniqueness
That you fell in love with.
But you didn't think I was worthy
And now I offer myself all the love
That I craved, begged, and pleaded for.
You will regret it all and be consumed,
It is all that you deserve!

I never questioned anything when I was with you.
I never questioned who you were,
I never questioned who I was,
I never questioned what WE were.
It was the comfortability that never needed to be questioned.

Now I question everything.

I was certain about you.
I am still certain about you.
I will always be certain about you.
That's the thing about love...
My feelings tell me everything
My head won't allow!

I'm not forcing this anymore.
I'm just going to be me,
Finally.
You will either simply fade away
Or
You will truly fight to stay.
One way or another,
It will prove whether you're the one.
Whether I was right or wrong.

When Night Falls

The Poetic Rants and
Ramblings
of a Lonely Broken Heart.

Top review from United Kingdom

Emma P

★★★★★ Verified Purchase

A thoughtful, painful insight into lost love.

Reviewed in the United Kingdom on 19 December 2021

Brutally honest and thoughtful poetry about the feelings of losing love. Highly recommended for lovers of poetry. I look forward to more.

Kelly-Marie Eadington

www.ingramcontent.com/pod-product-compliance
Lightning Source LLC
Chambersburg PA
CBHW070554160726
48003CB00005B/2039